Amazing life

BUGS AND SPIDERS

by George C. McGavin

An Hachette UK Company
www.hachette.co.uk

First published in the USA in 2013 by TickTock, an imprint of Octopus Publishing Group Ltd
Endeavour House, 189 Shaftesbury Avenue, London, WC2H 8JY
www.octopusbooks.co.uk www.octopusbooksusa.com
Copyright © Octopus Publishing Group Ltd 2013
Distributed in the US by Hachette Book Group, USA, 237 Park Avenue, New York, NY 10017, USA
Distributed in Canada by Canadian Manda Group, 165 Dufferin Street, Toronto, Ontario, Canada M6K 3H6

ISBN 978 1 84898 859 0

Printed and bound in China
10 9 8 7 6 5 4 3 2 1

With thanks to Marjorie Frank
Natural history consultant: Dr. Kim Dennis-Bryan F.Z.S
US Editor: Jennifer Dixon   Cover design: Steve West   Production Controller: Alexandra Bell

Picture credits (t=top; b=bottom; c=center; l=left; r=right):
FLPA: 14cl, 16tl, 16 main, 17t, 21tr, 21br, 24, 25, 28 main, 29. Nature Picture Library: 7cl, 7r, 11b, 15cl, 22c, 22b, 27t, 30b.
NHPA: 11t, 27b. Shutterstock: OFC, 1, 2, 3, 4, 5, 6, 7t, 8, 9, 10, 11cr, 12tl, 13, 14tl, 14ct, 14b, 15t, 15cr, 15c, 15bl, 15br, 17b, 18,
19, 20tl, 20–21 main, 22tl, 23, 26, 28tl, 30tl, 31, OBC. TickTock image archive: map page 12, 14cr.

Contents

Words that look
bold like this
are in the glossary.

What is an insect?

Insects are a group of animals that include bees, butterflies, ants, and beetles. All insects have six legs and a body in three parts. The sections of an insect's body are called the head, **thorax**, and **abdomen**.

Bugs can be tiny, like an ant, or big, like this giant grasshopper.

Insects have a pair of "feelers," called **antennae**, on their head.

Insects use their antennae to smell, touch, and find out what is going on around them.

Antenna

Head

Thorax

This is a close-up photo of an ant.

Abdomen

Leg

AMAZING INSECT FACT

There are more types of insects on Earth than any other animal. There are about one million different insects!

A dragonfly

Many bugs, such as dragonflies, have two pairs of wings. Others have one pair of wings, and some insects have no wings.

A fly has one pair of flight wings.

A flea has no wings.

This fly's eye is made of hundreds of tiny hexagonal shapes.

Eye

Insects have "compound" eyes. Their eyes are made of many small light-gathering sections.

5

Insect life

Most butterflies have a strawlike tongue for sipping nectar.

Some insects eat only plants. Others hunt and eat other insects. Wasps, bees, and butterflies are attracted to brightly colored flowers, where they drink a sweet juice called **nectar**.

Many bugs eat dead wood from rotting trees. The young, or **larvae**, of stag beetles eat rotting wood.

Adult stag beetle

Some insects, such as ants, live in big **colonies**. Others, such as adult stag beetles, live alone. Adult males and females get together to **mate**.

AMAZING INSECT FACT
Some beetles use flashes of light, made by special parts under their body, to attract a mate.

The female aphid in this photo is giving birth.

A firefly

Female moths produce special smells to attract mates. After mating, the female moth lays lots of eggs. She then leaves the eggs to hatch on their own.

A ruby tiger moth lays eggs on a leaf.

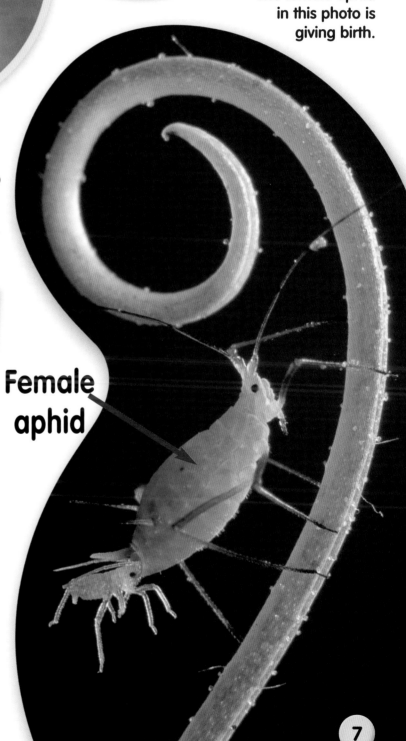

Female aphid

Some bugs, such as aphids, give birth to live young.

What is a spider?

Spiders belong to an animal group called arachnids. All spiders have four pairs of legs and a body in two parts. Spiders are **predators**. They hunt and eat other animals for food.

Tarantulas are big hairy spiders. They use some of the hairs to sense food and predators.

Leg

The spider's abdomen contains its **digestive organs** and the special glands, or body parts, that make silk for building webs.

Abdomen

The spider's head and thorax are joined together. This front part of its body is called the prosoma.

Prosoma

Pedipalps

Spiders have two small projections called pedipalps. They use them for feeling things.

Some spiders build webs. They make them out of silk threads. The threads come out of a part of the spider's body called the spinneret.

Web

Orb web spider

Eyes

AMAZING SPIDER FACT
Most spiders have eight eyes. All spiders have **fangs** for injecting poison into their **prey**.

This jumping spider has caught a fly and is holding it using its fangs.

Spider life

There are about 42,000 different types of spiders. Webs are a good sign that spiders are around. Webs made by orb spiders can be found on plants, on fences, and inside buildings.

Considering how thin it is, spider silk is very strong!

Some spiders sit in the middle of the web waiting for prey to arrive.

Other spiders stay out of sight, and when their web begins to shake, they know an insect has become trapped in it.

The spider wraps its prey in silk.

AMAZING SPIDER FACT
Spider silk is liquid (runny) until it comes out of the spinneret.

This is a tree trunk trapdoor spider.

Trapdoor spiders make underground **burrows** with a door above. When the spider senses something moving close to the door, it opens the trap door and pulls its prey down into the hole.

Burrow

Trapdoor

Eggs

Adult spiders live on their own. Males and females only get together to mate. After mating, the female spider lays lots of eggs and covers them with silk.

Many female spiders leave their eggs. The baby spiders, or spiderlings, hatch and have to take care of themselves.

This nursery web spider carries her eggs with her in a silk egg sac.

Egg sac

11

Insect and spider habitats

A habitat is the place where a plant or an animal lives. Insects live in habitats from hot **deserts** to cold mountains. Spiders live in lots of habitats, too, but not in very cold places, such as the Arctic or Antarctica.

There can be 2,000 different bugs living in a garden.

The ocean is a habitat, but no insects or spiders live in the ocean.

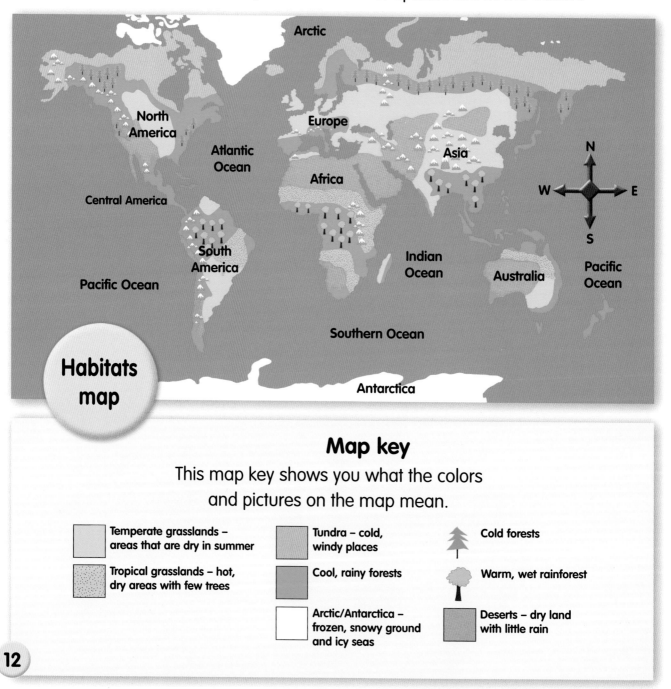

Habitats map

Arctic

North America

Atlantic Ocean

Europe

Asia

Africa

Central America

South America

Pacific Ocean

Indian Ocean

Australia

Pacific Ocean

Southern Ocean

Antarctica

N
W E
S

Map key
This map key shows you what the colors and pictures on the map mean.

Temperate grasslands – areas that are dry in summer

Tropical grasslands – hot, dry areas with few trees

Arctic/Antarctica – frozen, snowy ground and icy seas

Tundra – cold, windy places

Cool, rainy forests

Cold forests

Warm, wet rainforest

Deserts – dry land with little rain

Many insects, such as dragonflies, live in or near **freshwater** ponds, rivers, and lakes.

Dragonflies lay their eggs in ponds.

Leaf-cutter ants grow a **fungus** on the leaves they collect. The ants eat the fungus.

Leaf-cutter ants live in South American rainforests.

AMAZING INSECT FACT
Rainforests have more insects than any other habitat in the world.

One of the reasons there are so many insects and spiders is because they are small animals and do not need much habitat in which to live.

Hundreds of different types of insects can live on one oak tree.

What is a life cycle?

A life cycle is all the different **stages** and changes that a plant or animal goes through in its life. The diagrams on these pages show an example of an insect life cycle and a spider life cycle.

Sometimes a female spider thinks a male is prey in her web and eats him!

1

A male and female ladybug meet and mate.

LADYBUG LIFE CYCLE
Many insects have a life cycle with these stages.

2

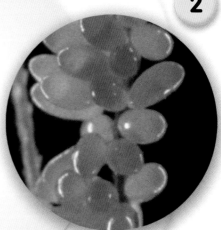

The female ladybug lays lots of eggs. She doesn't look after the eggs or her babies.

4

Inside the case the larva turns into an adult ladybug. This ladybug has just climbed out of its pupal case.

3

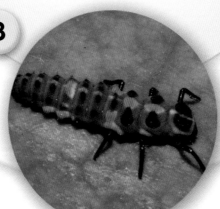

A larva hatches from each egg. The larva eats lots of aphids. Then the larva makes a case around its body and becomes a pupa.

1

An adult male and female spider meet and mate.

4

SPIDER LIFE CYCLE
Many spiders have a life cycle with these stages.

2

The spiderlings molt – their old skin falls off and a new skin underneath expands and hardens to fit the spider's larger size. They molt four or five times before they are fully grown.

3

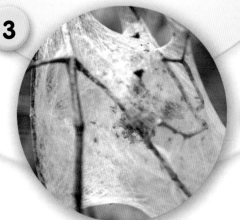

The female lays her eggs in a silk egg sac. Some spiders guard their eggs, while others leave them.

The spiderlings hatch. Some spiderlings make a tangled web. The spiderlings grow bigger. Their hard outer skin gets too small.

Praying mantid

Amazing insect and spider life cycles

Jumping spider

In this book we are going to find out about some amazing life cycles – from praying mantids to jumping spiders.

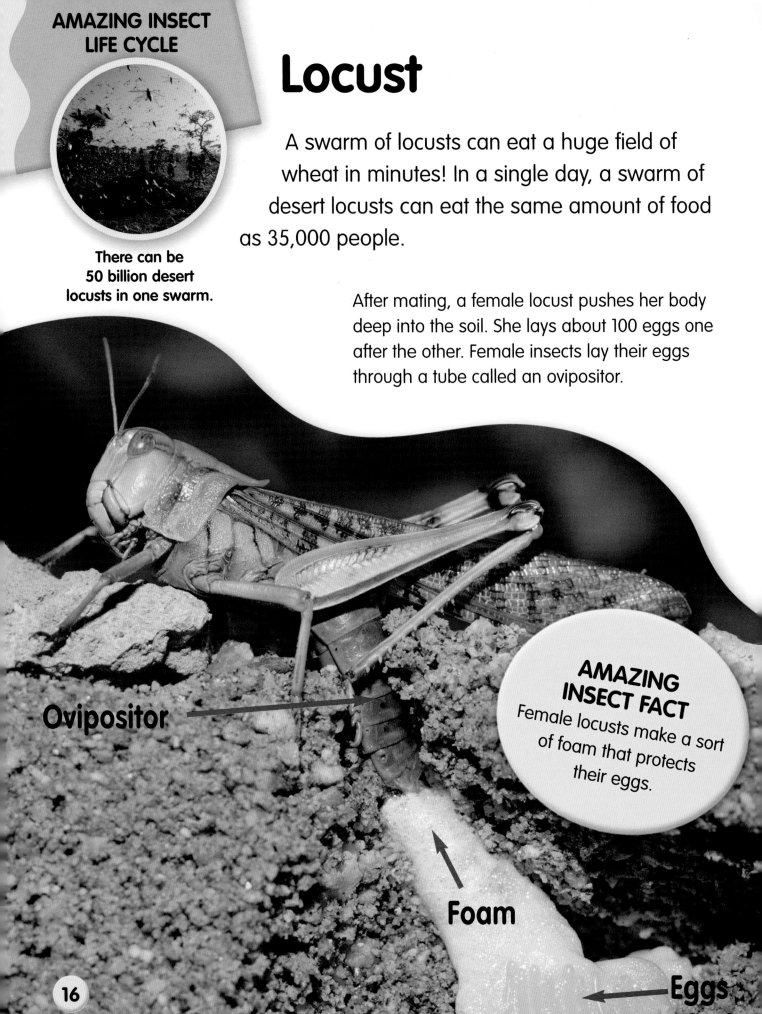

There can be
50 billion desert
locusts in one swarm.

Locust

A swarm of locusts can eat a huge field of wheat in minutes! In a single day, a swarm of desert locusts can eat the same amount of food as 35,000 people.

After mating, a female locust pushes her body deep into the soil. She lays about 100 eggs one after the other. Female insects lay their eggs through a tube called an ovipositor.

Ovipositor

AMAZING INSECT FACT
Female locusts make a sort of foam that protects their eggs.

Foam

Eggs

Tiny locust larvae called nymphs or hoppers hatch from the eggs.

Hopper

Large groups of hoppers are called bands. As they march along, they eat all the plants in their path.

As the hoppers grow, their skin becomes too tight. It splits and drops off. This is called molting. There is a new skin underneath.

Adult locust

After they have molted five times, the young hoppers become adults with wings.

Wing

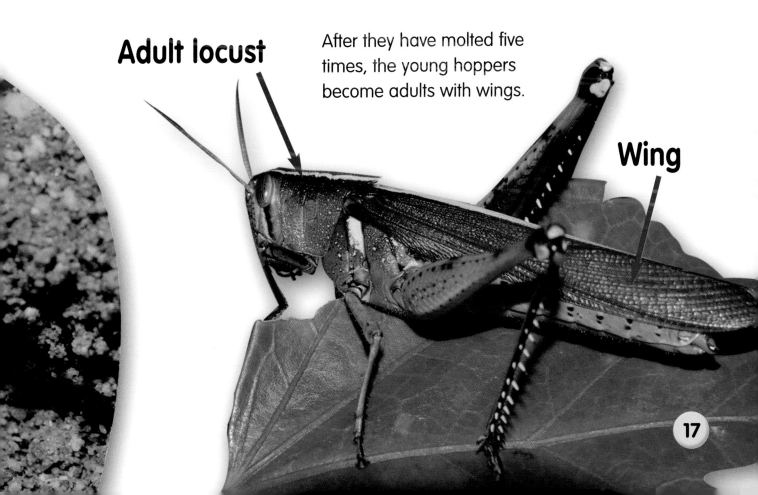

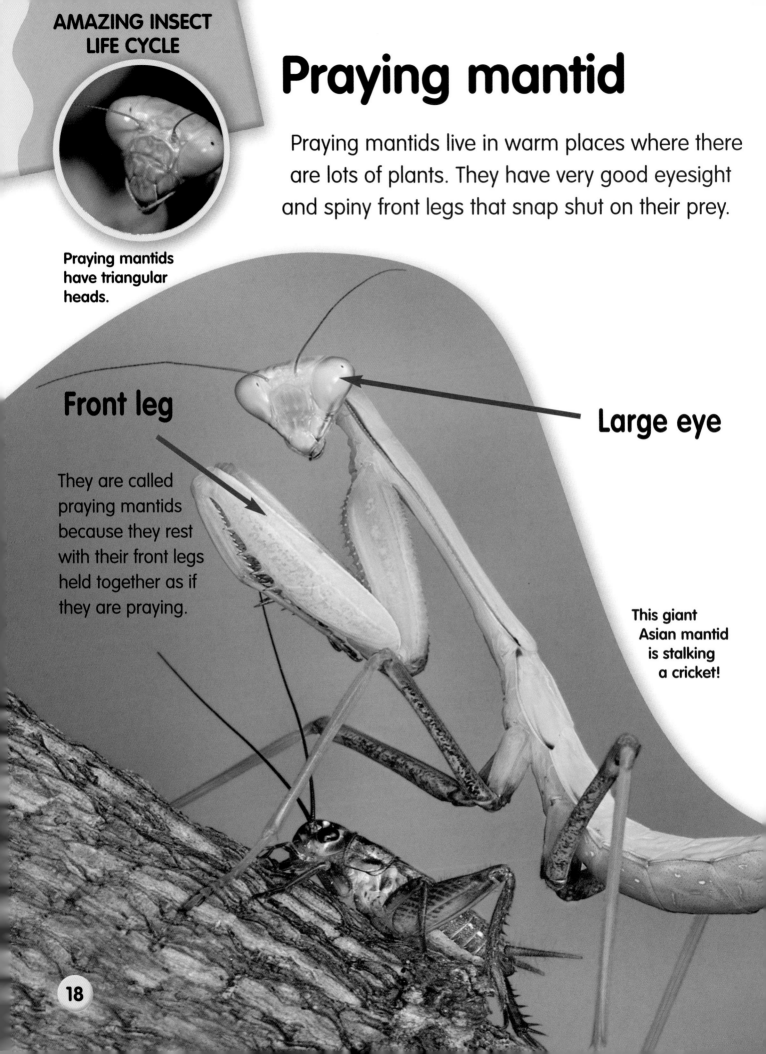

Praying mantids have triangular heads.

Praying mantid

Praying mantids live in warm places where there are lots of plants. They have very good eyesight and spiny front legs that snap shut on their prey.

Front leg

Large eye

They are called praying mantids because they rest with their front legs held together as if they are praying.

This giant Asian mantid is stalking a cricket!

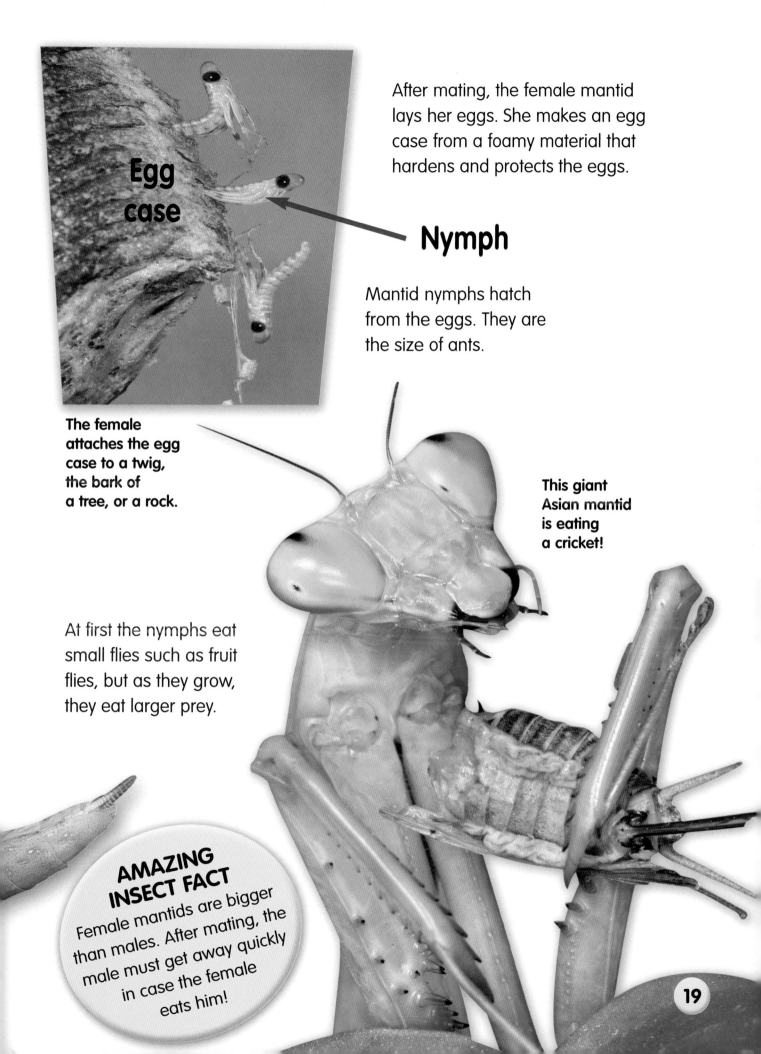

Egg case

After mating, the female mantid lays her eggs. She makes an egg case from a foamy material that hardens and protects the eggs.

Nymph

Mantid nymphs hatch from the eggs. They are the size of ants.

The female attaches the egg case to a twig, the bark of a tree, or a rock.

This giant Asian mantid is eating a cricket!

At first the nymphs eat small flies such as fruit flies, but as they grow, they eat larger prey.

AMAZING INSECT FACT
Female mantids are bigger than males. After mating, the male must get away quickly in case the female eats him!

Rhinoceros beetle

The rhinoceros, or rhino, beetle lives in rainforests. This beetle gets its name from its horn, which looks like a rhino's horn!

Only male rhino beetles have a horn.

This rhino beetle is two inches (five centimeters) long.

AMAZING INSECT FACT
Adult rhino beetles feed on nectar, rotting fruit, and **sap** from trees and plants.

Male rhino beetles sometimes use their horns to fight over **territory** with other males. If the male has a good territory with plenty of food, he will be able to attract a female.

After mating, the female rhino beetle lays her eggs. The eggs hatch into larvae. After two to three years, each larva becomes a **pupa**.

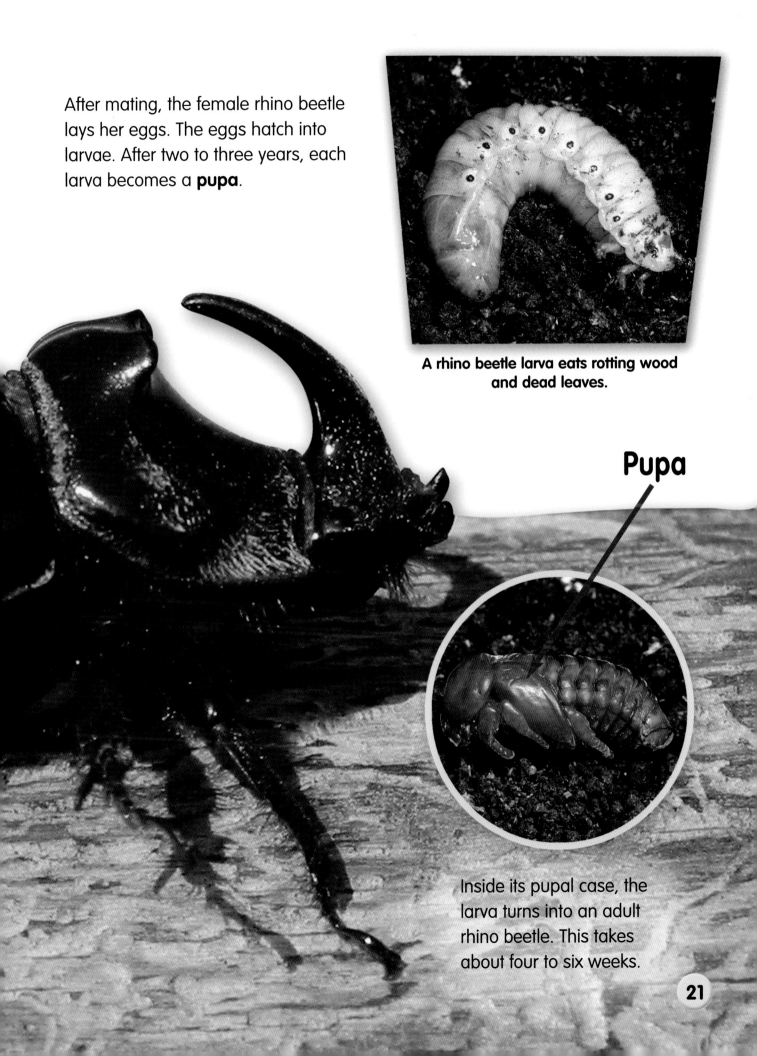

A rhino beetle larva eats rotting wood and dead leaves.

Pupa

Inside its pupal case, the larva turns into an adult rhino beetle. This takes about four to six weeks.

All butterflies have two pairs of wings.

Birdwing butterfly

Butterflies live in lots of different habitats – from rainforests to city gardens. There are about 17,500 different types of butterflies. The Queen Alexandra birdwing is the biggest butterfly in the world.

The male and female Queen Alexandra birdwing butterflies look different from each other. The female is bigger than the male.

Male

11 in. (28 cm)

This butterfly's wingspan is bigger than the wingspan of some birds!

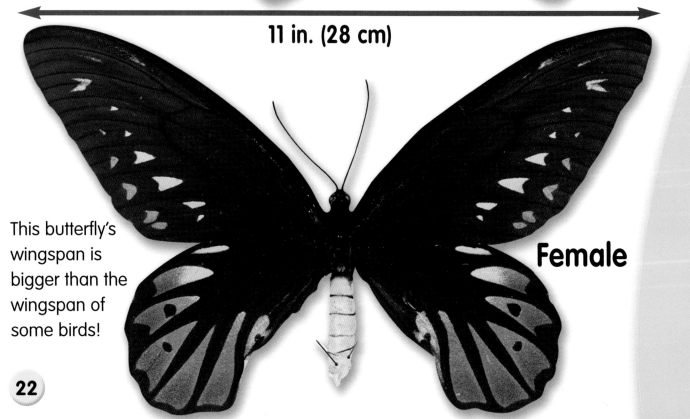

Female

22

All butterflies have the same kind of life cycle.

A male and female butterfly meet and mate. The female lays lots of eggs. Larvae, called caterpillars, hatch from the eggs. They eat and eat.

This is a monarch butterfly caterpillar.

The caterpillar gets too big for its skin. The old skin molts and there's a new skin underneath. The caterpillar molts several times.

This photo shows the caterpillar making its case.

Then the caterpillar makes a case around its body and becomes a pupa.

AMAZING INSECT FACT
The Queen Alexandra birdwing butterfly lives only in Papua New Guinea, in South East Asia.

Inside the pupal case, the caterpillar becomes a butterfly!

This monarch butterfly is crawling out of its case.

23

A spider-hunting wasp sting can be very painful to humans.

Spider-hunting wasp

There are about 4,000 different types of spider-hunting wasps in the world. The female wasp will fly above the ground or run around tapping the ground with her antennae hunting for spiders.

When the female wasp catches a spider, she fights with the spider and stings it so it is paralyzed. This means it cannot move, but it is still alive.

Antenna

Wings

Wolf spider

Burrow

The wasp then drags the spider to a burrow she has dug and pulls the spider underground.

The paralyzed spider cannot escape!

AMAZING INSECT FACT

Some types of spider-hunting wasps are three inches (seven centimeters) long! Most types are under one inch (25 millimeters) long.

The female lays a single egg on the spider and then seals the burrow. When the egg hatches, the young wasp larva eats the spider alive!

The wasp larva spins a silk case called a cocoon. Inside the cocoon it becomes an adult wasp. The new adult wasp crawls to the surface and escapes from the burrow.

Most jumping spiders have hairy bodies.

Jumping spider

Jumping spiders live in forests, in woodland, in gardens, and in many other habitats around the world. There are about 5,000 different types of jumping spiders.

Jumping spiders have eight eyes – two of the eyes are very big, like car headlights. The spider's big eyes help it to spot its insect prey and judge the distance of its jump.

Jumping spiders jump to catch prey and to escape from predators, such as birds.

The jumping spider in this photo is pouncing on a hoverfly. The spider attaches a safety line of silk in case it misses its landing spot.

Silk safety line

Hoverfly

AMAZING SPIDER FACT
The jumping spider can leap up to 25 times the length of its own body!

This female has hidden her egg sac in a dead leaf.

After mating, the female jumping spider lays lots of eggs all at once. She wraps them in an egg sac made of silk thread.

Most females guards their eggs until the spiderlings hatch.

Large water spiders eat baby fish and tadpoles.

Water spider

The water spider lives underwater in ponds or slow-flowing rivers. It lives in a diving bell, like a bubble, made out of silk, which it fills with air.

The spider sits inside the diving bell. When prey, such as an insect, passes, the spider rushes out, grabs the prey, and takes it back to the bell to eat.

The spider sits with just its front legs dangling in the water. Its head is in the bell so it can breathe.

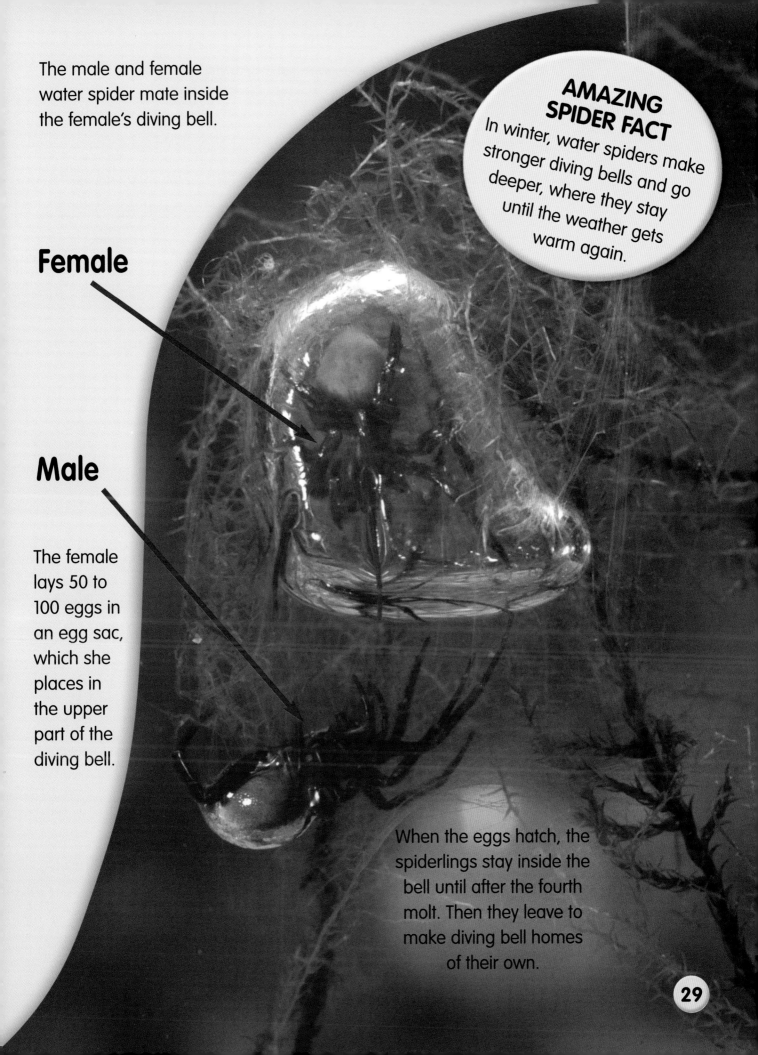

The male and female water spider mate inside the female's diving bell.

Female

Male

The female lays 50 to 100 eggs in an egg sac, which she places in the upper part of the diving bell.

AMAZING SPIDER FACT
In winter, water spiders make stronger diving bells and go deeper, where they stay until the weather gets warm again.

When the eggs hatch, the spiderlings stay inside the bell until after the fourth molt. Then they leave to make diving bell homes of their own.

That's amazing!

Most insects and spiders do not look after their eggs or young, but there are some amazing insect and spider parents. These good moms feed their babies and protect them from being eaten by predators.

The wolf spider carries her spiderlings on her back.

A female earwig looks after her eggs inside an underground burrow. She licks them every day to stop fungus from growing on them.

Insects such as bees and wasps live in large groups and make a nest in which to look after their young.

Earwig

Eggs

Cell

Egg

Paper wasp

Paper wasps make a nest of papery chewed-up wood.

A female queen bee or wasp lays all the eggs. An egg is laid in each cell of the nest. Larvae hatch from the eggs.

The other females in the group, called workers, help to look after the nest and feed the larvae.

AMAZING INSECT FACT
Female paper wasps feed their larvae on chewed-up insects.

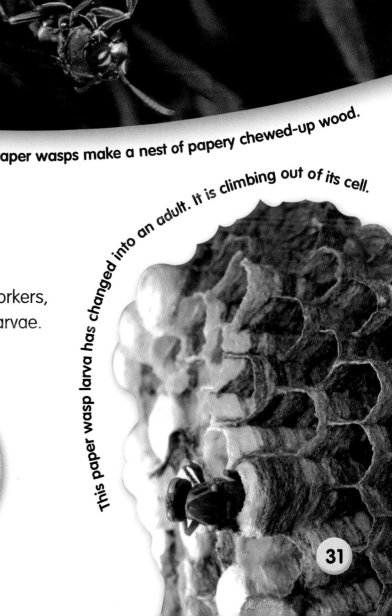

This paper wasp larva has changed into an adult. It is climbing out of its cell.

Glossary

abdomen – The part of an animal's body that contains the digestive organs, heart, and reproductive organs.

antennae – A pair of "feelers" used by an insect to touch and smell its environment.

burrows – Tunnels and holes under the ground where some animals live.

colonies – Large groups.

desert – A place where it hardly ever rains. Most deserts are very hot in the day. Some deserts get cold at night.

digestive organs – The body parts that digest food, such as the stomach.

fangs – Very sharp toothlike structures.

freshwater – Rainwater and the water in ponds and some rivers. It is not salty.

fungus – A very simple living thing that grows and spreads. Another word we use for some types of fungus is mold.

larvae – The young of some insects.

mate – When a male and female animal meet and have babies.

nectar – A sweet liquid produced by flowers to attract insects.

predators – Animals that hunt and kill other animals for food.

prey – Animals that are hunted by other animals as food.

pupa – The stage in the life cycle of some insects between a larva and an adult.

sap – A liquid in trees and plants.

stages – Different times of an animal's life when the animal changes.

territory – An area or place that an animal defends and where the animal feeds and breeds.

thorax – The middle part of an insect's body. The legs and wings are attached to the thorax.

Index